PUFFIN BOOKS

Editor: Kaye Webb

THE PUFFIN SONG BOOK

LESLIE WOODGATE

THE
PUFFIN SONG BOOK

COMPILED AND ARRANGED BY
LESLIE WOODGATE

PENGUIN BOOKS

Penguin Books Ltd, Harmondsworth, Middlesex, England
Penguin Books Inc. 7110 Ambassador Road, Baltimore, Maryland 21207, U.S.A.
Penguin Books Australia Ltd, Ringwood
Victoria, Australia
—

Published in Puffin Books 1956
Reprinted 1961, 1963, 1965, 1967, 1970
—

Made and printed in Great Britain
by Lowe & Brydone (Printers) Ltd

Cover design by Ronald Searle

Illustrations by Heather Standring

This book is sold subject to the condition
that it shall not, by way of trade or otherwise,
be lent re-sold, hired out, or otherwise circulated
without the publisher's prior consent in any form of
binding or cover other than that in which it is
published and without a similar condition
including this condition being imposed
on the subsequent purchaser

FOREWORD

MUSIC-MAKING is one of the happiest ways of employing spare time and is one of the few things you can enjoy either alone or with others. I have therefore chosen some songs I have known since childhood, and others which I came to know and love at school. Some are in French and German, and as songs are universal they may open the door to friendship in a wonderful fashion when you are away from home.

As a boy, I used to sing with my brothers and sisters, and one of our special favourites was Tallis' canon 'Glory to thee my God this night', which we often sang in bed before we went to sleep. That was how we learnt to sing in two parts.

Playing the piano with another person is always good fun, so I have arranged some settings as piano duets. Neither part is difficult, but you must decide whether you play first or second according to your own ability.

I have given other songs recorder accompaniments, and I hope some of the tunes I have added to the voice parts will be enjoyed both by player and listener. Don't be afraid of the violin obligatos; they are very simple and add something to the whole effect.

A few songs have percussion parts, to which you can add or subtract other instruments as you wish. The main thing is to play with *good rhythm* so that the song swings along happily.

There are some arrangements for three-part voices which I thought might be suitable for choirs. To join in with a group of keen singers is a most rewarding experience, and the songs I have arranged have interesting parts for each voice.

Whether you sing indoors or out, you will find something in this book for the mood and the moment. There are some old favourites, and some new songs which you probably won't know at all, but which I am sure will soon rank as great favourites with you, as they are with me.

LESLIE WOODGATE

ACKNOWLEDGEMENTS

I am grateful to the following for allowing me to use arrangements which are their copyright: J. B. Cramer & Co. Ltd for 'Twankydillo'; J. Curwen & Sons Ltd for 'Blow Away the Morning Dew' and 'The Farmer's Daughters'; Novello & Co. Ltd for 'O Soldier won't you marry me?' and 'Hark the Herald Angels Sing'.

CONTENTS

Foreword	v
Acknowledgements	vi
Ah! vous dirai-je, maman (*piano duet*)	138
Aiken Drum (*tambourine, drum, and piano*)	128
Alouette (*piano*)	32
Au clair de la lune (*violin*)	25
Away in a manger (*recorder and piano*)	185
Baa baa black sheep (*piano*)	108
Bells of Aberdovey, The (*bells and piano*)	60
Blow away the morning dew (*piano*)	48
Blow the wind southerly (*violin and piano*)	135
Cockles and mussels (*recorder and piano*)	67
Cock Robin (*piano*)	94
Come follow me (*round*)	47
Coventry Carol, The (*voices*)	181
Curly locks (*piano*)	140
Dame, get up and bake your pies (*recorder*)	88
Deck the hall with holly (*three voices or voice and piano*)	168
Die Lorelei (*piano*)	14
Ding dong bell (*voices*)	153
Drink to me only with thine eyes (*three voices*)	44
Farmer's daughters, The (*piano*)	106
Fire down below (*piano duet*)	123
First Nowell, The (*piano*)	176
Frère Jacques (*piano or bells*)	20
Frog he would a-wooing go, A (*piano*)	104

Girls and boys come out to play (*piano*)	2
Glory to thee my God this night (*piano*)	16
God that madest earth and heaven (*voices*)	6
Good King Wenceslas look'd out (*piano*)	126
Great Tom (*round*)	63
Greensleeves (*recorder*)	28
Hark the herald angels sing (*piano*)	188
Haste thee, nymph (*round*)	37
Heidenröslein (*piano*)	18
Hickory, dickory, dock (*piano*)	149
Hieland laddie (*cymbals, drum, and piano*)	164
Hunting horn, The (*round*)	141
Hush-a-bye baby (*piano duet*)	150
I got a robe (*piano*)	58
I had a little nut-tree (*piano*)	152
Il était une bergère (*recorder and piano*)	101
I saw three ships (*piano*)	22
Jésus Christ s'habille en pauvre (*piano*)	4
Jingle bells (*jingles, triangle, piano, and bass*)	70
Jolly miller, The (*piano*)	30
Keel row, The (*piano duet*)	112
Lavender's blue (*two voices*)	12
Little Bo-peep (*piano*)	66
London Bridge (*piano*)	116
London's burning (*round*)	134
Lord's Prayer, The (*piano*)	8
Lubin Loo (*piano*)	142

Magnificat (*voices*) 186
Malbrouk s'en va-t-en guerre (*drum, cymbal, piano, and toy trumpet*) 38
Mary, Mary, quite contrary (*two voices*) 90
Mrs Bond (*recorder and piano*) 42
Mulberry bush, The (*piano duet*) 76
My bonnie is over the ocean (*piano*) 118
My dame hath a lame tame crane (*round*) 137
My pretty maid (*piano*) 172

New-born King, The (*nativity play*) 175
Nobody knows the trouble I've seen (*piano*) 74
Nut-brown maiden, The (*piano*) 46

Old John Braddleum (*piano*) 81
Old King Cole (*violin and piano*) 132
Old MacDonald had a farm (*piano*) 84
One man went to mow (*voices*) 51
Oranges and lemons (*bells and piano*) 96
O soldier won't you marry me? (*piano*) 78
Over the hills and far away (*piano*) 56

Polly put the kettle on (*piano*) 34

Quittez pasteurs (*recorder and piano*) 120

Richard of Taunton Dene (*piano*) 85

St Paul's steeple (*piano*) 148
Sandmännchen (*piano*) 52
She'll be coming round the mountain (*piano*) 50
Sing a song of sixpence (*piano*) 1
Swing low, sweet chariot (*piano*) 10

There was a lady loved a swine (*piano*)	26
There was an old woman tossed up in a basket (*violin and piano*)	35
Three blind mice (*with* Frère Jacques) (*round*)	115
Turn again Whittington (*round*)	80
Twankydillo (*triangle, drum, and piano*)	143
Westminster bells (*round*)	147
We three kings of Orient are (*recorder and piano*)	183
What are little boys made of? (*piano*)	100
When Johnny comes marching home (*cymbals, drum, and piano*)	91
While shepherds watched their flocks by night (*piano*)	180
White sand and grey sand (*round*)	17
Widdecombe Fair (*piano*)	109
Wiegenlied (*piano*)	64
Zion's children (*tambourine, triangle, drum, piano duet*)	154
Index of first lines	191

All accompaniments are arranged by Leslie Woodgate except those for 'Wiegenlied' (p. 64) and 'Heidenröslein' (p. 18), by Schubert and 'Sandmännchen' (p. 52) by Brahms.

SING A SONG OF SIXPENCE

2. The king was in the counting house counting out his money,
   The queen was in the parlour eating bread and honey.
   The maid was in the garden hanging out the clothes,
   When by came a blackbird and snapped off her nose!

GIRLS AND BOYS COME OUT TO PLAY

JÉSUS CHRIST S'HABILLE EN PAUVRE

2. 'Les miettes de notre table
   Nos chiens les mangeront bien.
   Ils nous rapportent des lièvres,
   Toi, tu ne m'apportez rien.'

3. 'Madame, qu'êtes en fenêtre,
   Faites-moi la charité!'
   'Ah! montez, montez, bon pauvre,
   Avec moi vous souperez.'

4. Après qu'ils êurent soupé,
   Il demande à se coucher.
   'Ah! montez, montez, bon pauvre,
   Un lit frais vous trouverez.'

5. Comme ils montaient les degrés
   Trois beaux anges les éclairaient
   'Ah! ne craignez rien, Madame,
   C'est la lune qui parait.'

6. Dans trois jours vous mourerez,
   En Paradis vous irez,
   Et votre mari, Madame,
   En enfer ira brûler!

A French carol of the 15th century

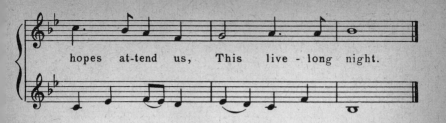

2. Guard us sleeping, guard us waking,
   And when we die,
   May we in thy mighty keeping
   All peaceful lie:
   When the last dread call shall wake us,
   Do not thou our God forsake us,
   But to reign in glory take us
   With thee on high.

COME FOLLOW ME

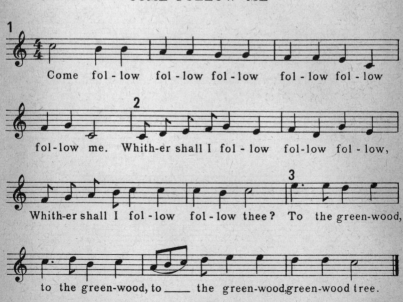

THE LORD'S PRAYER

ROBERT STONE
(1516-1613)

Robert Stone was a Tudor composer. The manuscript of his setting of 'The Lord's Prayer' is in the Bodleian Library, Oxford.

SWING LOW, SWEET CHARIOT

2. I'm sometimes up and sometimes down,
   Coming for to carry me home,
   But still my soul feels heavenly bound,
   Coming for to carry me home,
   Swing low, etc.

A negro spiritual, founded on the story of Elijah going to heaven in a fiery chariot

LAVENDER'S BLUE

3. Den Schiffer im kleinen Schiffe
Ergreift es mit wildem Weh,
Er schaut nicht die Felsenriffe,
Er schaut nur hinauf in die Höh'!
Ich glaube, die Wellen verschlingen
Am Ende Schiffer und Kahn;
Und das hat mit ihrem Singen
Die Lorelei getan.

A well known poem, founded on Greek mythology, by the German author Heinrich Heine

GLORY TO THEE MY GOD THIS NIGHT

THOMAS KEN
(1637-1711)

THOMAS TALLIS
(c. 1505-1585)

The melody is in canon, that is, one voice begins and a second comes in with the same tune a few beats later.

2. Forgive me, Lord, for thy dear Son,
   The ill that I this day have done,
   That with the world, myself, and Thee,
   I, ere I sleep, at peace may be.

3. Teach me to live, that I may dread
   The grave as little as my bed;
   Teach me to die that so I may
   Rise glorious at the awful day.

4. O may my soul on thee repose,
   And with sweet sleep mine eyelids close,
   Sleep that may me more vigorous make
   To serve my God when I awake.

5. When in the night I sleepless lie,
   My soul with heavenly thoughts supply;
   Let no ill dreams disturb my rest,
   No powers of darkness me molest.

6. Praise God, from whom all blessings flow,
   Praise him, all creatures here below,
   Praise him above, ye heavenly host,
   Praise Father, Son, and Holy Ghost.

WHITE SAND AND GREY SAND

HEIDENRÖSLEIN

Schubert wrote more than 600 songs. This is one of his best-known.

FRÈRE JACQUES

I SAW THREE SHIPS

AU CLAIR DE LA LUNE

2. Au clair de la lune
   Pierrot répondit:
   Je n'ai pas de plume,
   Je suis dans mon lit.
   Va chez la voisine,
   Je crois qu'elle y est,
   Car, dans sa cuisine,
   On bat le briquet.

3. Au clair de la lune
   Pierrot se rendort,
   Il rêve à la lune,
   Son cœur bat bien fort:
   Car toujours si bonne
   Pour l'enfant tout blanc,
   La lune lui donne
   Son croissant d'argent!

One of the best-known early French songs.

THERE WAS A LADY LOVED A SWINE

GREENSLEEVES

2. If you intend thus to disdain,
   It does the more enrapture me,
   And even so, I still remain
   A lover in captivity.
       Greensleeves etc.

3. Alas, my love, that you should own
   A heart of wanton vanity,
   So I must meditate alone
   Upon your insincerity.
       Greensleeves etc.

A song well known in Shakespeare's day. He mentions it in his play *The Merry Wives of Windsor.*

2. I love my mill, she is to me
    Both parent, child, and wife;
  I would not change my station for
    Another one in life.
  Then push, push, push the bowl my boys,
    And pass it round to me;
  The longer we sit here and drink
    The merrier we shall be.

3. Thus like the miller, bold and free,
    Let us rejoice and sing.
  The days of youth were made for glee,
    And time is on the wing.
  This song shall pass from me to thee,
    Around this jovial ring,
  Let heart and voice and all agree
    To sing 'Long live the King.'

A popular song of the 17th century.

ALOUETTE

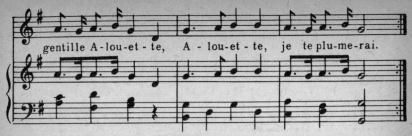

1. Alouette, gentille Alouette,
   Alouette, je te plumerai.
   Je te plumerai la tête,
   Je te plumerai la tête,
   À la tête, à la tête,
   Alouette.

2. Alouette, gentille Alouette,
   Alouette, je te plumerai.
   Je te plumerai le bec,
   Je te plumerai le bec,
   À le bec, à le bec,
   À la tête, à la tête,
   Alouette.

3. Alouette, gentille Alouette,
   Alouette, je te plumerai.
   Je te plumerai les yeux,
   Je te plumerai les yeux.
   À les yeux, à les yeux,
   À le bec, à le bec,
   À la tête, à la tête,
   Alouette.

4. Alouette, gentille Alouette,
   Alouette, je te plumerai.
   Je te plumerai les ailes,
   Je te plumerai les ailes,
   À les ailes, à les ailes,
   À les yeux, à les yeux,
   À le bec, à le bec,
   À la tête, à la tête,
   Alouette.

5. Alouette, gentille Alouette,
   Alouette, je te plumerai.
   Je te plumerai le dos,
   Je te plumerai le dos.
   À le dos, à le dos,
   À les ailes, à les ailes,
   À les yeux, à les yeux,
   À le bec, à le bec,
   À la tête, à la tête,
   Alouette.

6. Alouette, gentille Alouette,
   Alouette, je te plumerai.
   Je te plumerai les jambes,
   Je te plumerai les jambes.
   À les jambes, à les jambes,
   À le dos, à le dos,
   À les ailes, à les ailes,
   À les yeux, à les yeux,
   À le bec, à le bec,
   À la tête, à la tête,
   Alouette.

7. Alouette, gentille Alouette,
   Alouette, je te plumerai.
   Je te plumerai les pieds,
   Je te plumerai les pieds.
   À les pieds, à les pieds,
   À les jambes, à les jambes,
   À le dos, à le dos,
   À les ailes, à les ailes,
   À les yeux, à les yeux,
   À le bec, à le bec,
   À la tête, à la tête,
   Alouette, gentille Alouette,
   Alouette, je te plumerai.

A French-Canadian folksong

POLLY PUT THE KETTLE ON

THERE WAS AN OLD WOMAN TOSSED UP IN A BASKET

The melody is called 'Lilliburlero' and is said to have been written by Henry Purcell (1658-1695)

HASTE THEE, NYMPH

JOHN MILTON
(1608-1674)

SAMUEL ARNOLD
(1740-1802)

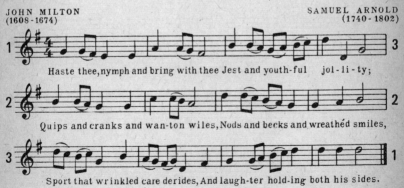

MALBROUK S'EN VA-T-EN GUERRE

2. Il reviendra z'à Pâques,
   Ou à la Trinité.
   La bas, courez, etc.

3. La Trinité se passe,
   Marlbrouck ne revient pas.
   La bas, courez, etc.

4. Madame à sa tour monte,
   Si haut qu'elle peut monter.
   La bas, courez, etc.

5. Elle aperçoit son page,
   Tout de noir habillé.
   La bas, courez, etc.

6. Beau page, ah! mon beau page,
   Quell' nouvelle apportez?
   La bas, courez, etc.

7. Aux nouvelles que j'apporte
   Vos beaux yeux vont pleurer.
   La bas, courez, etc.

8. Monsieur Malbrouk est mort,
   Est mort et enterré!
   La bas, courez, etc.

9. Je l'ai vu porter en terre
   Par quatre z'officiers.
   La bas, courez, etc.

A French marching song

MRS BOND

2. 'John Ostler, go fetch me a duckling or two;
   John Ostler, go fetch me a duckling or two;
   Cry dilly, dilly, dilly, dilly, come and be killed,
   For you must be stuff'd, and my customers filled!'

3. 'I have been to the ducks that are swimming in the pond,
   And they won't come to be killed, Mrs Bond;
   I cried dilly, dilly, dilly, dilly, come and be killed,
   For you must be stuff'd, and the customers filled!'

4. Mrs Bond she went down to the pond in a rage,
   With plenty of onions and plenty of sage;
   She cried, 'Come, little wag-tails, come, and be killed,
   For you shall be stuff'd, and my customers filled!'

2. I sent thee late a rosy wreath,
   Not so much hon'ring thee,
   As giving it a hope, that there
   It could not wither'd be;
   But thou thereon didst only breathe
   And sent'st it back to me,
   Since when it grows and smells, I swear,
   Not of itself but thee!

THE NUT-BROWN MAIDEN

J. STUART BLACKIE
(1809-1895)

*hiri = pronounce hee-ree

2. O Mary, mild eyed Mary,
   By land or on the sea,
   Though time and tide may vary
   My heart beats true to thee.
      Horo etc.

3. And when, with blossom laden,
   Bright summer comes again,
   I'll fetch my nut-brown maiden
   Down frae the bonnie glen.
      Horo etc.

A Gaelic song well known in the Highlands of Scotland

BLOW AWAY THE MORNING DEW

2. She gathered up her lovely flowers
   And spent her time in sport,
   As if in pretty Cupid's bowers
   She daily did resort.
   And sing etc.

3. The yellow cowslip by the brim,
   The daffodil as well,
   The timid primrose, pale and trim,
   The pretty snow-drop bell.
   And sing etc.

4. She's gone with all those flowers sweet
   Of white, of red, of blue,
   And unto me, about my feet,
   Is only left the rue.
   And sing etc.

A Somerset folksong

SHE'LL BE COMING ROUND THE MOUNTAIN

2. She'll be driving six white horses when she comes
3. O we'll all go out to meet her when she comes
4. We will kill the old red rooster when she comes
5. And we'll all have chicken and dumpling when she comes

A popular American song

ONE MAN WENT TO MOW

Four men went to mow, etc.
(up to as many as you have patience for!)

SANDMÄNNCHEN

*Voice II by Leslie Woodgate

Brahms is one of the greatest of all song writers. This is a charming lullaby.

2. Die Vögelein, sie sangen so süss im Sonnenschein,
   Sie sind zur Ruh gegangen in ihre Nestchen klein.
   Das Heimchen in dem Ährengrund, es tut allein sich kund:
   Schlafe, schlafe - schlaf du, mein Kindelein!

3. Sandmännchen kommt geschlichen und guckt durchs Fensterlein,
   Ob irgend noch ein Liebchen nicht mag zu Bette sein.
   Und wo er nun ein Kindchen fand, streut er ihm in die Augen Sand.
   Schlafe, schlafe - schlaf du, mein Kindelein!

4. Sandmännchen aus dem Zimmer, es schläft mein Herzchen fein,
   Es ist gar fest verschlossen schon sein Guckäugelein.
   Es leuchter morgen mir Willkomm das Äugelein so fromm!
   Schlafe, schlafe - schlaf du, mein Kindelein!

OVER THE HILLS AND FAR AWAY

OVER THE HILLS AND FAR AWAY

2. Tom with his pipe made such a noise
   That he pleased both the girls and boys,
   And they stopped to hear him play
   'Over the hills and far away.'
   Over the hills and a great way off,
   The wind shall blow my topknot off.

A well known English Nursery Rhyme. The melody was used by John Gay in 'The Beggar's Opera'.

I GOT A ROBE

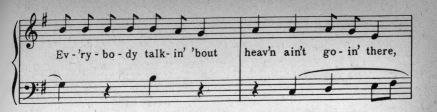

2. I got-a shoes, you got-a shoes,
   All of God's children got-a shoes,
   When I get to heaven goin' to put on my shoes,
   Goin' to walk all over God's heaven, heaven, heaven.
   Ev'rybody talkin' 'bout heav'n ain't goin' there.
   Heaven, heaven, goin' to walk all over God's heaven.

3. I got-a harp, you got-a harp,
   All of God's children got-a harp,
   When I get to heaven goin' to play on my harp,
   Goin' to play all over God's heaven, heaven, heaven.
   Ev'rybody talkin' 'bout heav'n ain't goin' there.
   Heaven, heaven, goin' to play all over God's heaven.

A negro spiritual

THE BELLS OF ABERDOVEY

DUNCAN YOUNG (1902-)

Part of the melody appears in an opera *'Liberty Hall'* by Charles Dibdin (1745-1814). The original song was sung by a Welsh comedian. His few native words included the six chimes of the Aberdovey bells: *Un, dau, tri, pedwar, pump, chwech.*

GREAT TOM

'Great Tom' hangs in the tower built by Sir Christopher Wren, Christ Church, Oxford.

WIEGENLIED

2. Schlafe, schlafe in dem süssen Grabe,
   Noch beschütz dich deiner Mutter Arm,
   Alle Wünsche, alle Habe
   Fasst sie liebend, alle Liebewarm.

3. Schlafe, schlafe in der Flaumen Schosse,
   Noch umtönt dich lauter Liebeston,
   Eine Lilie, eine Rose,
   Nach dem Schlafe werd' sie dir zum Lohn.

One of Schubert's charming melodies

LITTLE BO-PEEP

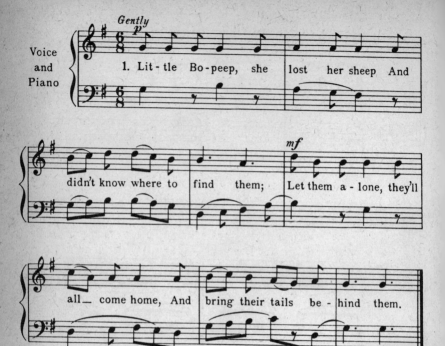

2. Little Bo-peep fell fast asleep,
   And dreamt she heard them bleating;
   But when she awoke, she found it a joke,
   For they were still a-fleeting.

3. Then up she took her little crook,
   Determined for to find them,
   She found them indeed but it made her heart bleed,
   For they'd left their tails behind them.

4. It happened one day as Bo-peep did stray
   Into a meadow hard by,
   There she espied their tails side by side,
   All hung on a tree to dry.

5. She heaved a sigh and wiped her eye,
   Then went o'er hill and dale,
   And tried what she could, as a shepherdess should,
   To tack to each sheep its tail.

COCKLES AND MUSSELS

2. She was a fishmonger, but sure 'twas no wonder,
   For so were her father and mother before,
   And they each wheeled their barrow thro' streets broad and narrow
   Crying 'Cockles and Mussels! alive, alive, O!'
   Alive, alive, O! alive, alive, O!
   Crying 'Cockles and Mussels! alive, alive, O!'

3. She died of a fever, and no one could save her,
   And that was the end of sweet Molly Malone,
   But her ghost wheels her barrow thro' streets broad and narrow
   Crying 'Cockles and Mussels! alive, alive, O!'
   Alive, alive, O! alive, alive, O!
   Crying 'Cockles and Mussels! alive, alive, O!'

A popular Irish song, 18th century

JINGLE BELLS

2. A day or to ago
   I thought I'd take a ride,
   And soon Miss Fanny Bright,
   Was seated by my side.
   The horse was lean and lank,
   Misfortune seemed his lot,
   He got into a drifted bank
   And we, we got upset.
       Jingle bells, etc.

3. Now the ground is white,
   Go it while you're young;
   Take the girls tonight,
   And sing this sleighing song.
   Just get a bobtailed bay,
   Two-forty for his speed,
   Then hitch him to an open sleigh,
   And crack! you'll take the lead.
       Jingle bells, etc.

An American song

NOBODY KNOWS THE TROUBLE I'VE SEEN

A negro spiritual

THE MULBERRY BUSH

2. This is the way we dry our hands, etc.
3. This is the way we clap our hands, etc.
4. This is the way we brush our teeth, etc.
5. This is the way we comb our hair, etc.
6. This is the way the ladies walk, etc.
7. This is the way the gentlemen walk, etc.

Actions can be made for each verse.

O SOLDIER, WON'T YOU MARRY ME?

An old English folksong, words and melody collected by Cecil J. Sharp (1859-1924)

TURN AGAIN WHITTINGTON

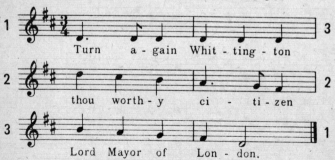

OLD JOHN BRADDLEUM

Number four, some thinks nowt but thinks the more.
Number five, some folks die when they can't keep alive.
Number six, some use crutches when they can't use sticks.
Number seven, some likes t'other place, give I heaven.
Number eight, some folks drink till they can't walk straight.
Number nine, some drinks beer 'cos they can't get wine.
Number ten, there bean't no women where there bean't no men.
Number eleven, much 'bout same as number seven.
Number twelve, if you want any more you can sing it yourself.

OLD MACDONALD HAD A FARM

3. pigs (grunt, grunt)
4. sheep (baa, baa)
5. cows (moo, moo)

RICHARD OF TAUNTON DENE

*imitating horse's hooves

2. Miss Jean she came without delay
   To hear what young Dicky had got to say;
   'I s'pose you do know me, Mistress Jean,
   I'm honest Richard of Taunton Dene.'
       Singing dumbledum etc.

3. 'I'm honest, though I be but poor,
   I never was in love before;
   My mother bade me come to woo,
   And I can fancy none but you.'
       Singing dumbledum etc.

4. 'Suppose that I should be your bride,
   Pray how would you for me provide?
   For I can neither sew nor spin;
   Pray what would your day's work bring in?'
       Singing dumbledum etc.

5. 'Why I can plough and I can sow,
   And sometimes I to market go
   With Farmer Johnson's straw and hay,
   And I earn my ninepence every day.'
       Singing dumbledum etc.

6. 'Ninepence a day will never do,
   For I must have silks and satins too;
   Ninepence a day won't buy us meat.'
   'Adzooks,' says Dick, 'I've a sack of wheat.'
       Singing dumbledum etc.

7. Dick's compliments did so delight,
   They made the family laugh outright.
   Young Richard took huff, no more would say,
   He kicked up old Dobbin and rode away.
       Singing dumbledum etc.

A Somerset folksong

DAME, GET UP AND BAKE YOUR PIES

3. Dame, what makes your ducks to die,
   Ducks to die, ducks to die?
   Dame, what makes your ducks to die
   On Christmas Day in the morning?

4. Their wings are cut, they cannot fly,
   Cannot fly, cannot fly;
   Their wings are cut, they cannot fly,
   On Christmas Day in the morning.

MARY, MARY, QUITE CONTRARY

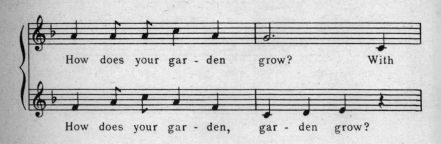

WHEN JOHNNY COMES MARCHING HOME

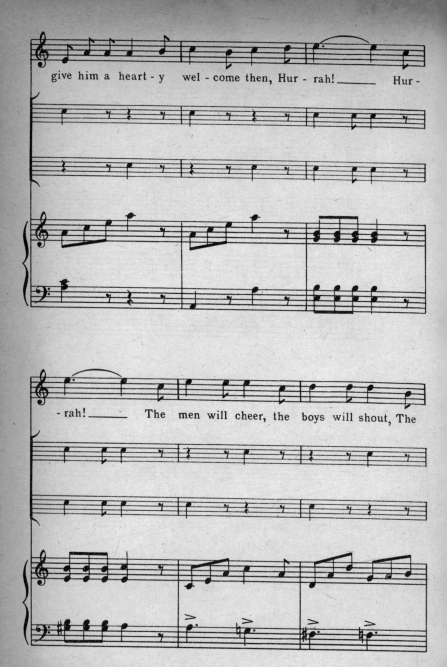

2. Get ready for the Jubilee,
   Hurrah! Hurrah!
   We'll give the hero three times three,
   Hurrah! Hurrah!
   The laurel wreath is ready now
   To place upon his royal brow,
   And we'll all feel gay when Johnny comes marching home.

3. Let love and friendship on that day
   Hurrah! Hurrah!
   Their best of treasure then display.
   Hurrah! Hurrah!
   And let each one perform his part
   To fill with joy the warrior's heart,
   And we'll all feel gay when Johnny comes marching home.

COCK ROBIN

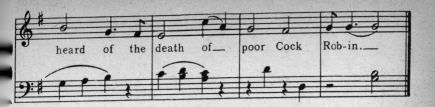

2. Who saw him die?
    I, said the fly,
    With my little eye,
    I saw him die.
       All the birds etc.

3. Who'll dig his grave?
    I, said the owl,
    With my little trowel,
    I'll dig his grave.
       All the birds etc.

4. Who'll toll the bell?
    I, said the bull,
    Because I can pull,
    I'll toll the bell.
       All the birds etc.

5. Who'll be the parson?
    I, said the rook,
    With my bell and book,
    I'll be the parson.
       All the birds etc.

6. Who'll be chief mourner?
    I, said the dove,
    I'll mourn for my love,
    I'll be chief mourner.
       All the birds etc.

Each character should be sung by one voice

ORANGES AND LEMONS

Pancakes and fritters, say the bells of St Peter's.
Two sticks and an apple, say the bells of Whitechapel.
Old Father Baldpate, say the slow bells of Aldgate.
Poker and tongs, say the bells of St John's.
Kettles and pans, say the bells of St Ann's.
Brickbats and tiles, say the bells of St Giles'.

Here comes a candle to light you to bed,
And here comes a chopper to cut off your head.
Chop chop etc.

This old nursery rhyme is supposed to mention all the bell-towers in the square mile of the City of London.

WHAT ARE LITTLE BOYS MADE OF?

IL ÉTAIT UNE BERGÈRE

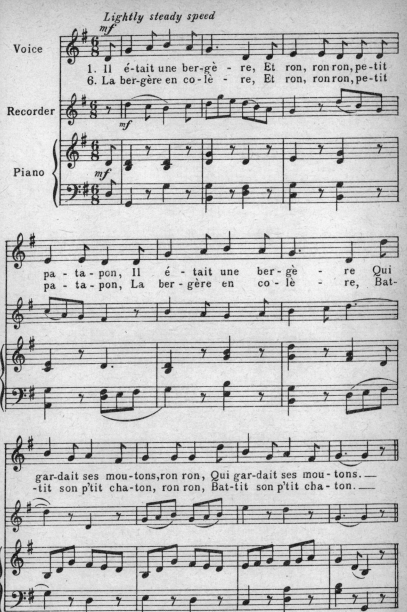

A French popular song

A FROG HE WOULD A-WOOING GO

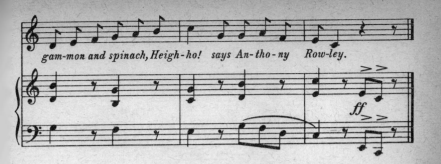

gam-mon and spinach, Heigh-ho! says An-tho-ny Row-ley.

2. Off he set with his opera hat,
   And on the road he met with a rat.

3. Soon they arrived at the mouse's hall,
   They gave a loud tap and they gave loud call.

4. 'Pray, Mrs Mouse, are you within?'
   'Yes, kind Sir! I'm sitting to spin.'

5. 'Pray, Mrs Mouse, will you give us some beer?
   That Froggy and I may have good cheer.'

6. 'Pray, Mr Frog, will you give us a song?
   Let the subject be something that's not over long.'

7. 'Indeed, Mrs Mouse!' replied the Frog,
   'A cold has made me as hoarse as a hog.'

8. 'Since you have caught cold, Mr Frog', Mousy said,
   'I'll sing you a song that I have just made.'

9. As they were in glee and merrymaking,
   A cat and her kittens came tumbling in.

10. The cat she seized the rat by the crown,
    The kittens they pulled the little mouse down.

11. This put Mr Frog in a terrible fright,
    He took up his hat and he wished them good-night.

12. As Froggy was crossing it over a brook,
    A lily-white duck came and gobbled him up.

13. So here is an end of one, two, and three,
    The rat, the mouse, and the little Froggy.

THE FARMER'S DAUGHTERS

2. One day they walked by the river's brim,
   When the eldest pushed the youngest in.

3. 'O sister, O sister, pray lend me your hand,
   And I'll give you both house and land.'

4. 'I'll neither lend you hand nor glove,
   Unless you promise me your true love.'

5. So down the river the maiden swam,
   Until she came to the miller's dam.

6. The miller's daughter stood at the door,
   Blooming like a gillyflower.

7. 'O Father, O Father, here comes a swan
   Very much like a gentlewoman!'

8. The miller he took his rod and hook,
   And he fished the maiden out of the brook.

A west country folksong

BAA BAA BLACK SHEEP

WIDDECOMBE FAIR

2. And when shall I see again my grey mare?
     All along, down along, out along lee.
   By Friday soon or Saturday noon,
     With Bill Brewer, etc.

3. Then Friday came and Saturday noon,
     All along, down along, out along lee.
   But Tom Pearce's old mare hath not trotted home,
     With Bill Brewer, etc.

4. So Tom Pearce he got to the top of the hill,
     All along, down along, out along lee.
   And he see'd his old mare down a-making her will,
     With Bill Brewer, etc.

5. So Tom Pearce's old mare her took sick and died,
     All along, down along, out along lee.
   And Tom he sat down on a stone and he cried,
     With Bill Brewer, etc.

6. But this isn't the end o' this shocking affair,
     All along, down along, out along lee.
   Nor, tho' they be dead, of the horrid career
     Of Bill Brewer, etc.

7. When the wind whistles cold on the moor of a night
     All along, down along, out along lee.
   Tom Pearce's old mare doth appear ghastly white,
     With Bill Brewer, etc.

8. And all the night long be heard skirling and groans
     All along, down along, out along lee.
   From Tom Pearce's old mare in her rattling bones,
     With Bill Brewer, etc.

A popular Devon song

THE KEEL ROW

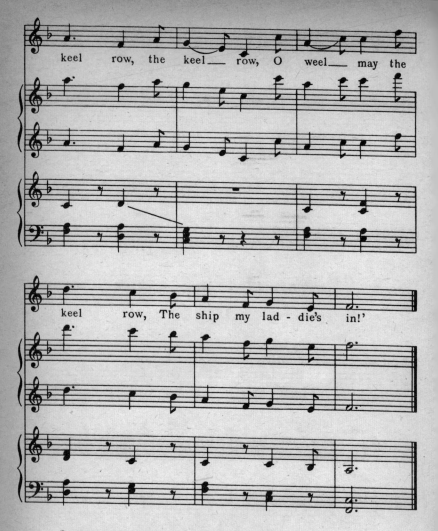

2. My love he wears a bonnet, a bonnet, a bonnet,
   A snawy rose upon it, a dimple in his chin.
       'O weel etc.

3. And soon I heard her lover, her lover, her lover,
   Had landed from the Rover, and joined her in this strain.
       'O weel etc.

A folksong from Newcastle, Northumberland

THREE BLIND MICE with FRÈRE JACQUES

LONDON BRIDGE
(1st version)

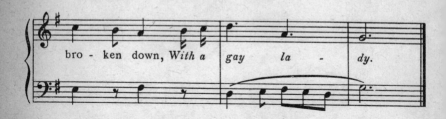

2. How shall we build it up again?
3. Silver and gold will be stole away.
4. Build it up with iron and steel.
5. Iron and steel will bend and bow.
6. Build it up with wood and clay.
7. Wood and clay will wash away.

last verse:
Build it up with stone so strong,
Dance over my Lady Lee,
Huzza! 'twill last for ages long
With a fair lady.

LONDON BRIDGE
(2nd version)

2. Build it up with iron bars.
3. Iron bars will bend and break.
4. Build it up with gold and silver.
5. Gold and silver I've not got.
6. Here's a prisoner I have got.
7. What's the prisoner done to you?
8. Stole my watch and broke my chain.
9. What'll you take to set him free.
10. One hundred pounds will set him free?
11. One hundred pounds we have not got.
12. Then off to prison he must go.

MY BONNIE IS OVER THE OCEAN

2. O blow ye winds over the ocean,
   O blow ye winds over the sea,
   O blow ye winds over the ocean,
   And bring back my bonnie to me.
      Bring back etc.

3. Last night as I lay on my pillow,
   Last night as I lay on my bed,
   Last night as I lay on my pillow,
   I dreamed that my bonnie was dead.
      Bring back etc.

4. The winds have blown over the ocean,
   The winds have blown over the sea,
   The winds have blown over the ocean,
   And brought back my bonnie to me.
      Brought back etc.

QUITTEZ, PASTEURS

Dieu Qui vient vous con - so - ler.

2. Vous le verrez
   Couché dans une étable,
   Comme un enfant
   Nu, pauvre, et languissant,
   Reconnaissez
   Son amour ineffable
   Pour nous venir chercher
   Il est, il est, il est,
   Le fidèle berger!

3. Rois d'Orient,
   L'étoile vous éclaire;
   À ce grand Roi
   Rendez hommage et foi,
   L'astre brillant
   Vous mène à la lumière
   De ce soleil naissant;
   Offrez, offrez, offrez,
   L'or, la myrrhe, et l'encens.

4. Esprit divin
   À qui tout est possible
   Percez nos cœurs
   De vos douces ardeurs;
   Notre destin
   Par vous devient paisible,
   Dieu prétend nous donner
   Le ciel, le ciel, le ciel,
   En venant s'incarner.

An old French carol

FIRE DOWN BELOW

2. Fire in the forepeak, fire down below,
   It's fetch a bucket of water, girls,
   There's fire down below.

3. Fire in the windlass, fire in the chain,
   It's fetch a bucket of water, girls,
   And put it out again.

4. Fire up aloft, and fire down below,
   It's fetch a bucket of water, girls,
   There's fire down below.

An old sea shanty

GOOD KING WENCESLAS LOOKED OUT

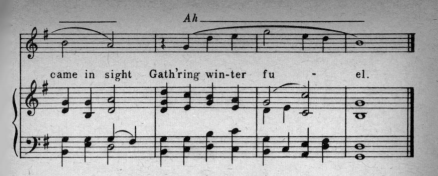

2. 'Hither, page, and stand by me,
    If thou know'st it, telling,
   Yonder peasant, who is he?
    Where and what his dwelling?'
   'Sire, he lives a good league hence,
    Underneath the mountain,
   Right against the forest fence,
    By Saint Agnes' fountain.'

3. 'Bring me flesh and bring me wine,
    Bring me pine logs hither:
   Thou and I will see him dine,
    When we bear them thither.'
   Page and monarch, forth they went,
    Forth they went together;
   Through the rude wind's wild lament
    And the bitter weather.

4. 'Sire, the night is darker now,
    And the wind blows stronger;
   Fails my heart, I know not how;
    I can go no longer.'
   'Mark my footsteps, good my page;
    Tread thou in them boldly:
   Thou shalt find the winter's rage
    Freeze thy blood less coldly.'

5. In his master's steps he trod,
    Where the snow lay dinted;
   Heat was in the very sod
    Which the Saint had printed.
   Therefore, Christian men, be sure,
    Wealth or rank possessing,
   Ye who now will bless the poor,
    Shall yourselves find blessing.

AIKEN DRUM

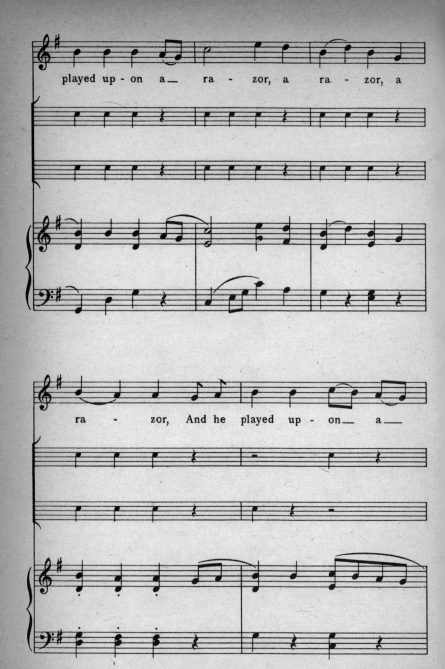

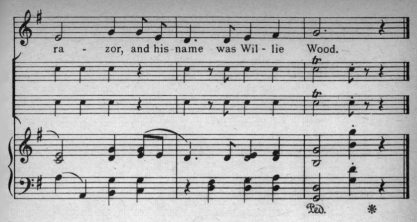

ra - zor, and his name was Wil - lie Wood.

2. His hat was made o' the guid roast beef, guid roast beef, guid roast beef,
His hat was made o' the guid roast beef, and his name was Willie Wood;
And he played upon a razor, a razor, a razor,
And he played upon a razor, and his name was Willie Wood.

3. His coat was made o' the haggis bag, the haggis bag, the haggis bag,
His coat was made o' the haggis bag, and his name was Willie Wood;
And he played upon a razor, a razor, a razor,
And he played upon a razor, and his name was Willie Wood.

4. His buttons were made o' the baubee baps, the baubee baps, the baubee baps,
His buttons were made o' the baubee baps, and his name was Willie Wood;
And he played upon a razor, a razor, a razor,
And he played upon a razor, and his name was Willie Wood.

5. But another man came to our town, to our town, to our town,
Another man came to our town, and his name was Aiken Drum;
And he played upon a ladle, a ladle, a ladle,
And he played upon a ladle, and his name was Aiken Drum.

6. And he ate up a' the guid roast beef, the guid roast beef, the guid roast beef,
And he ate up a' the guid roast beef, and his name was Aiken Drum;
And he played upon a ladle, a ladle, a ladle,
And he played upon a ladle, and his name was Aiken Drum.

7. And he ate up a' the haggis bags, the haggis bags, the haggis bags,
And he ate up a' the haggis bags, and his name was Aiken Drum;
And he played upon a ladle, a ladle, a ladle,
And he played upon a ladle, and his name was Aiken Drum.

8. And he ate up a' the baubee baps, the baubee baps, the baubee baps,
And he ate up a' the baubee baps, and his name was Aiken Drum;
And he played upon a ladle, a ladle, a ladle,
He played upon a ladle, and his name was Aiken Drum.

An old Scots nursery rhyme

OLD KING COLE

LONDON'S BURNING

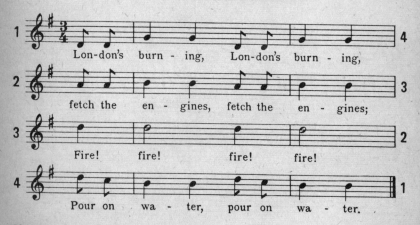

BLOW THE WIND SOUTHERLY

A north country folksong

MY DAME HATH A LAME TAME CRANE

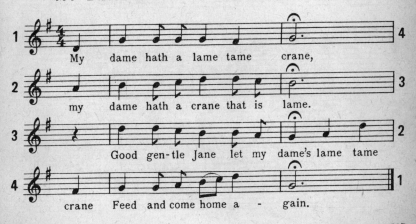

AH! VOUS DIRAI-JE, MAMAN

A well-known nursery tune, popular all over Europe

CURLY LOCKS

THE HUNTING HORN

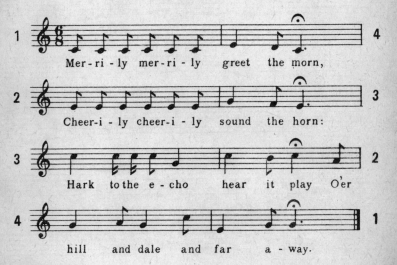

LUBIN LOO

TWANKYDILLO

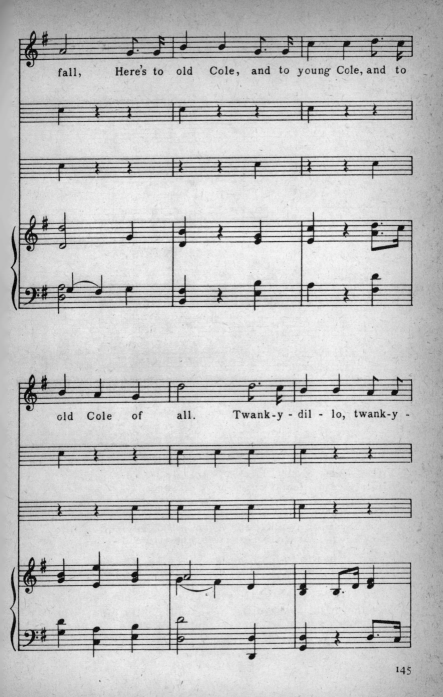

If a gentleman calls his horse for to shoe,
He makes no denial of one port or two,
For it makes my bright hammer to rise and to fall,
Here's to old Cole, and to young Cole, and to old Cole of all.

Twankydillo, twankydillo, twankydillo, dillo, dillo, dillo,
And he that loves strong beer is a hearty good fellow.

Here's a health to the King, and likewise his Queen,
And to all the royal little ones where'er they are seen,
Which makes my bright hammer to rise and to fall,
Here's to old Cole and to young Cole, and to old Cole of all.

Twankydillo, twankydillo, twankydillo, dillo, dillo, dillo,
A roaring pair of bagpipes made of the green willow.

A Sussex folksong

WESTMINSTER BELLS

ST PAUL'S STEEPLE

This refers to the old legend that an apple tree once sprouted on the top of St Paul's Cathedral.

HICKORY, DICKORY DOCK!

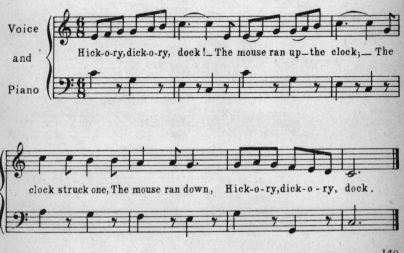

HUSH-A-BYE BABY

I HAD A LITTLE NUT-TREE

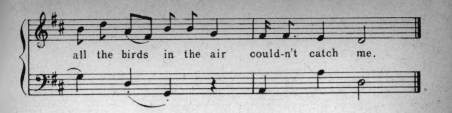

DING DONG BELL

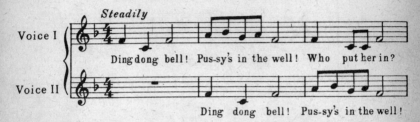
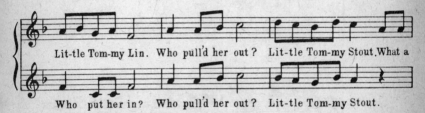
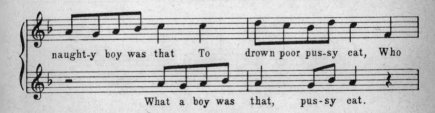
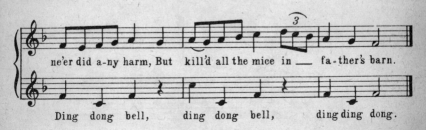

ZION'S CHILDREN

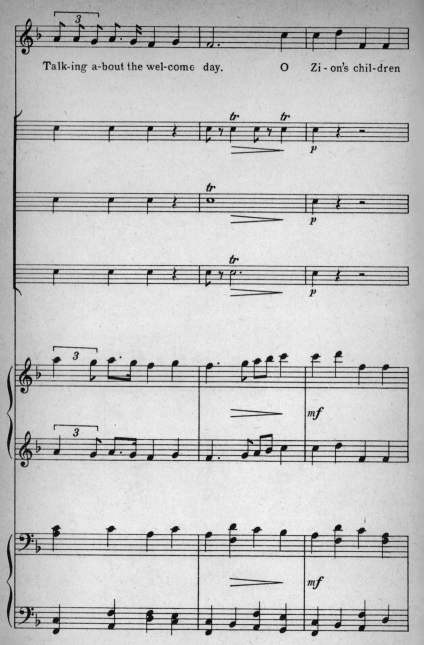

162

A negro spiritual sung by the Jubilee Singers of Fiske University (U.S.A.) in 1888

HIELAND LADDIE

2. When he drew his good broad sword,
   Bonnie laddie, hieland laddie,
   Then he gave his royal word,
   Bonnie laddie, hieland laddie,
   From the field he ne'er would flee,
   Bonnie laddie, hieland laddie,
   But with his friends would live or dee,
   Bonnie laddie, hieland laddie.

3. Weary fall the lowland loon,
   Bonnie laddie, hieland laddie,
   Who took from him the English crown.
   Bonnie laddie, hieland laddie.
   Blessings on the kilted clans,
   Bonnie laddie, hieland laddie,
   Who fought for him at Prestonpans,
   Bonnie laddie, hieland laddie.

The melody is used as a military march by the Scots Guards.

DECK THE HALL WITH HOLLY

THOMAS OLIPHANT
(1799-1873)

See page 171 for verses 2-3.

DECK THE HALL WITH HOLLY

2. See the flowing bowl before us,
   Strike the harp and join the chorus,
   Follow me in merry measure,
   While I sing of mirth and pleasure.

3. Fast away the Old Year passes,
   Hail the New, ye lads and lasses,
   Singing gaily all together
   Heedless of the wind and weather.

A Welsh carol for the New Year

MY PRETTY MAID

2. 'Shall I go with you, my pretty maid?
   Shall I go with you, my pretty maid?'
   'Yes, if you please, kind Sir,' she said,
   'Sir,' she said, 'Sir,' she said,
   'Yes, if you please, kind Sir,' she said.

3. 'What is your fortune, my pretty maid?
   What is your fortune, my pretty maid?'
   'My face is my fortune, Sir,' she said,
   'Sir,' she said, 'Sir,' she said,
   'My face is my fortune, Sir,' she said.

4. 'Then I can't marry you, my pretty maid,
   Then I can't marry you, my pretty maid.'
   'Nobody asked you, Sir,' she said,
   'Sir,' she said, 'Sir,' she said,
   'Nobody asked you, Sir,' she said.

Standring

THE NEW-BORN KING

NATIVITY PLAY

Angels, Kings, and Shepherds come to the place where Mary is with her child Jesus

CHARACTERS: Scene 1 – Shepherds and Angels
Scene 2 – Mothers nursing babies, Herod
Scene 3 – The Three Kings
Scene 4 – The Virgin Mary, Joseph

STAGE SETTING

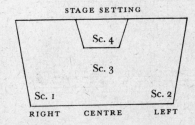

The First Nowell is sung before the curtain rises. As the curtain goes up, Shepherds are seen sitting on the right in front of a log fire. They sing *While Shepherds Watched*. An Angel appears and sings verses 2, 3, and 4, and verses 5 and 6 are sung by all. The stage darkens and on the left are seen, as the light gets brighter, several women nursing babies. All sing *The Coventry Carol* (Herod can stamp on to the stage and sing verse 2). The stage darkens and in centre stand the Three Kings (Melchior, Caspar, Balthazar). All sing verses 1 and 5 of *We Three Kings from Orient are*. Each King sings his particular verse (2, 3, and 4), and all sing the refrain. The stage darkens, and, built up, top centre of stage, appears the Crib, with the Virgin Mary, sitting, surrounded by Angels. Joseph stands by the side of the Crib. *Away in a Manger* is sung. Tableau of the Shepherds, Mothers, Kings, Virgin Mary, and Angels. Virgin Mary sings *Magnificat*. All sing *Hark, the Herald Angels Sing*.

CURTAIN

THE FIRST NOWELL

-ell, Born is the king of Is - ra - el!

3. And by the light of that same star,
   Three Wise Men came from country far;
   To seek for a king was their intent,
   And to follow the star wheresoever it went.
       Nowell, nowell, nowell, nowell,
       Born is the king of Israel!

4. This star drew nigh to the north-west;
   O'er Bethlehem it took its rest,
   And there it did both stop and stay
   Right over the place where Jesus lay:
       Nowell, etc.

5. Then entered in those Wise Men three,
   Fell reverently upon their knee
   And offered there in his presence
   Both gold and myrrh and frankincense:
       Nowell, etc.

6. Then let us all with one accord
   Sing praises to our heavenly Lord,
   That hath made heaven and earth of naught
   And with his blood mankind hath bought.
       Nowell, etc.

verse 3 as verse 1
verse 4 as verse 1
verse 5 as verse 2
verse 6 as verse 2

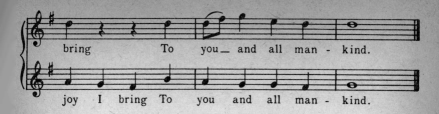

bring To you and all man-kind.

joy I bring To you and all man-kind.

3. 'To you in David's town this day
   Is born of David's line
   A Saviour who is Christ the Lord;
   And this shall be the sign:'

4. 'The Heavenly Babe you there shall find
   To human view displayed,
   All meanly wrapped in swathing bands
   And in a manger laid.'

5. Thus spake the seraph; and forthwith
   Appear'd a shining throng
   Of angels praising God, who thus
   Address'd their joyful song:

6. 'All glory be to God on high,
   And to the earth be peace;
   Good will henceforth from heaven to men
   Begin and never cease.'

verse 3 as verse 1
verse 4 as verse 2
verse 5 as verse 1
verse 6 as verse 2

THE COVENTRY CAROL

Solo 1. Lul-ly, lul-la, thou lit-tle ti-ny child,
By by, lul-ly lul-lay, thou lit-tle ti-ny child, By by, lul-ly lul-lay.

From the Coventry Pageant of the Shearmen and the Tailors (15th century)

AWAY IN A MANGER

WILLIAM JAMES KIRKPATRICK
(1838-1921)

2. The cattle are lowing, the baby awakes,
   But the little Lord Jesus no crying he makes.
   I love thee, Lord Jesus! Look down from the sky
   And stay by my bedside till morning is nigh.

3. Be near me, Lord Jesus, I ask thee to stay
   Close by me for ever, and love me, I pray;
   Bless all the dear children in thy tender care,
   And fit us for heaven, to live with thee there.

MAGNIFICAT

LESLIE WOODGATE

Words from the Authorised Version of the Bible, St. Luke, Chapter I, verses 46-55

HARK THE HERALD ANGELS SING

CHARLES WESLEY
(1707-1788)

FELIX MENDELSSOHN
(1809-1847)
Adapted by W.H.Cummings

2. Christ, by highest heav'n adored,
   Christ, the everlasting Lord,
   Late in time behold him come,
   Offspring of a Virgin's womb.
   Veiled in flesh the Godhead see!
   Hail, the incarnate Deity,
   Pleased as Man with man to dwell,
   Jesus, our Emmanuel!
       Hark the herald angels etc.

3. Hail, the heaven-born Prince of peace!
   Hail, the Sun of righteousness!
   Light and life to all he brings,
   Risen with healing in his wings.
   Mild he lays his glory by,
   Born that man no more may die,
   Born to raise the sons of earth,
   Born to give them second birth.
       Hark the herald angels etc.

INDEX OF FIRST LINES

A farmer he lived in the west country	106
A frog he would a woo-ing go	104
Ah! vous dirai-je, maman	138
Alas, my love you do me wrong	28
Alouette, gentille Alouette	32
As I came down thro' Sandgate	112
Au clair de la lune	25
Away in a manger, no crib for a bed	183
Baa, baa, black sheep, have you any wool?	108
Blow the wind southerly, southerly, southerly	135
Come follow, follow, follow	7
Curly locks, curly locks	140
Dame, get up and bake your pies	88
Dashing thro' the snow	70
Deck the hall with boughs of holly	168
Die Blümelein, sie schlafen schon	52
Ding dong bell	153
Drink to me only with thine eyes	44
Fire in the galley, fire down below	123
Frère Jacques, Frère Jacques	20
Gaily ringing o'er the dales	60
Girls and boys come out to play	2
Glory to thee, my God, this night	16
God that madest earth and heaven	6
Good King Wenceslas look'd out	126
Great Tom is cast	63

Hark the herald angels sing	188
Haste thee, nymph and bring with thee	37
Here's a health to the jolly blacksmith	143
Here we go Lubin Loo	142
Here we go round the mulberry bush	76
Hickory, dickory, dock!	149
Horo my nut-brown maiden	46
Hush-a-bye baby on the tree top	150
Ich weiss nicht was soll es bedeuten	14
I got a robe	58
I had a little nut-tree	152
Il était une bergère	101
In Dublin's fair city	67
I saw three ships come sailing by	22
Jésus Christ s'habille en pauvre	4
Last New Year's Day, as I've heard say	85
Lavender's blue, diddle diddle	12
Little Bo-Peep, she lost her sheep	66
London Bridge is broken down	116
London Bridge is falling down	117
London's burning	134
Lully, lulla, thou little tiny child	181
Malbrouk s'en va-t-en guerre	38
Mary, Mary, quite contrary	90
Merrily, Merrily, greet the morn	141
My bonnie is over the ocean	118
My dame hath a lame tame crane	137
My soul doth magnify the Lord	186

Nobody knows the trouble I've seen	74
Number one, number one	81
Old King Cole was a merry old soul	132
Old MacDonald had a farm	84
One man went to mow..	51
Oranges and lemons	96
O soldier won't you marry me?	78
Our Father which art in heaven	8
O, what have you got for dinner, Mrs Bond?	42
Polly put the kettle on	34
Quittez, pasteurs, vos brebis, vos houlettes	120
Sah ein Knab' en Röslein stehn	18
Schlafe, schlafe, holder süsser Knabe	64
She'll be coming round the mountain	50
Sing a song of sixpence, a pocket full of rye	1
Swing low, sweet chariot	10
The first Nowell the angel did say	176
The little bell at Westminster	147
There came a man to our town	128
There was a jolly miller once	30
There was a lady loved a swine	26
There was an old woman tossed up in a basket	35
Three blind mice (*with* Frère Jacques)	115
Tom he was a piper's son	56
Tom Pearce, Tom Pearce, lend me your grey mare ..	109
Turn again Whittington	80

Upon Paul's steeple stands a tree	148
Upon the sweetest summer time	48
We three kings of Orient are	183
What are little boys made of?	100
When Johnny comes marching home	91
Where are you going to, my pretty maid?	172
Where have you been all the day?	164
While shepherds watched their flocks by night	180
White sand and grey sand	17
Who killed Cock Robin?	94
Zion's children, coming along	154